HYDE

A GARDEN FOR

In 1992 the Trustees of Hyde Hall (sisting of 24 acres of garden and some ... acres of adjacent farmland to the RHS to provide a centre for its members in the East of England. The former owners, Dr Dick and Mrs Helen Robinson, formed the Trust in 1976 to ensure the future of the fine garden they had created on an exposed Essex hilltop. We are immeasurably grateful to Dr and Mrs Robinson. Their skill and far-sightedness have provided the Society and its members with a garden, renowned in particular for its superb roses and for an astonishing range of other plants, which will continue to bring pleasure and instruction to many more thousands of people in the future.

Sir Simon Hornby
PRESIDENT, RHS

Opposite: Magnolia sprengeri

Cover: The top pond with pontederias, water lilies and other moisture-loving plants

See Garden Plan, left (under flap)

1 The borders by the house, the top pond, the Jubilee Garden, the Deodar cedar and the beds around the lawn. 2 The Woodland Garden with the shade-loving and ericaceous plants. 3 The Gold Garden – where all the plants have gold or yellow in their foliage, flowers or fruit. 4 A mixed border of species and shrub roses interplanted with other trees, shrubs and bulbs. 5 A varied selection of modern climbing roses, ramblers, and bush roses. 6 A collection of tall and intermediate bearded irises and mixed borders with individual colour themes, including one central bed of peonies. 7 An area which gives winter colour in many different forms. 8 The lower pond and waterfall beds. 9 A large part of the National Collection of *Viburnum* with other contrasting trees and shrubs. 10 Selected dwarf and slow-growing conifers with a collection of snowdrops. 11 A formal setting for miniature roses. 12 This area includes a bed of South African bulbs and a collection of trees and shrubs, some rare. 13 Car park with a long-term planting of trees to provide shade and interest. 14 The Pig Park – contains the main part of the National *Malus* Collection, old and new English roses, magnolias and various trees and shrubs. 15 Planted with flowering trees and shrubs. 16 Standing ground for plants. 17 Hermione's, a quiet shady area and the old stable floor with its self-sown riches. 18 The Tea Yard – a paved area surrounded by interesting plants.

INTRODUCTION

In 1955 when Dr and Mrs Robinson came to Hyde Hall there were only six trees on the top of a windswept hill and no garden. If they had known then what they soon learned, it is very doubtful that the garden would have been made!

Catalpa bignonioides 'Aurea' in the sheltered Tea Yard

As areas around the house were cleared they were planted with anything available. A chance visit to an auction sale in Wickford market on a cold February day where Dr and Mrs Robinson bought about 60 trees, a few for as little as 50 pence each, formed the early framework of the garden.

The first major work was on the farm pond in front of the house which was surrounded by barbed wire and high hedges. This was cleared and the area was developed over the following years. At the time, Hanningfield reservoir was being constructed and York stone paving from the old barns was available for the paths.

At the back of the house under inches of grass, the Tudor brick floor of an old stable was discovered and this has now become naturalised with pulsatillas, anemones and aquilegias which obviously enjoy the old mortar.

Attempts to grow rhododendrons in hopelessly unsuitable, exposed conditions failed. So in 1963 a shelter belt of conifers was planted on the north-east of what had been an old orchard. The soil was improved and the pH lowered; as a result, rhododendrons and other ericaceous plants now grow happily in this area.

In the mid 1960s Dr and Mrs Robinson were invited to contribute to a series of BBC gardening radio programmes which they enjoyed immensely. Through these they met many well-known gardeners and journalists whose friendship and knowledge were to prove very helpful in developing the garden.

In the early days, as roses grew well in the heavy soil, many more were planted, but in the shade of the rapidly growing trees the roses gradually deteriorated. So the Robinsons made a decision to take in three acres of farmland facing south. The present rose garden was laid out in this new area, followed over a period of years by the waterfall bed, the shrub rose

An early summer storm frames the top pond late in the afternoon

border, the winter garden, the *Viburnum* beds and finally the perennial border.

In 1968 the Robinsons gave up keeping pigs and part of the area where they had been kept, now known as the Pig Park, was made available for planting together with a small paddock where Jersey cows had formerly grazed. A gift of cherry and crab-apple trees from the late Jack Matthews started off the planting in this area and later more *Malus* and a selection of other trees were added and, more recently, shrub roses planted to extend the flowering season.

Before the Robinsons retired from farming in 1974, a 12-acre area beside the Chase was grassed down for use as a car park where about 500 young trees had been planted the previous year. Two years later Dr and Mrs Robinson set up a Charitable Trust to ensure the future of the garden while continuing to be responsible for the day-to-day management.

The weather during 1987 caused two serious setbacks; in January and February, 15-ft (4.5m) snowdrifts caused major loss and damage and the October gale brought down or dislodged 50 per cent of the trees. However the majority were restaked and most have survived.

There are of course, several ways in which a visitor may walk round the garden. This booklet offers a route which will lead the visitor through the various sections numbered in the text and on the plan.

I

HOUSE, TOP POND, JUBILEE GARDEN AND LILAC BANK

Immediately to the left of the entrance from the yard is a corner containing tender plants – *Fremontodendron*, an *Arbutus menziesii* and others. To the right, the back walls of the garage are covered with climbing roses and *Clematis* and the small lawn, with its Deodar cedar planted in 1959, is edged with roses. *Betula* 'Silver Shadow' with its very fine, white bark is also prominent in this area.

The House, which is not open to visitors, dates back to the 18th century and is a typical Essex farmhouse of timber frame, lath and plaster. Its south-facing front provides a sheltering wall for another *Fremontodendron*, various *Ceanothus* including the 'Trewithen Blue' and many half hardy plants like the long-flowering *Coronilla glauca* which displays its light yellow, pea-like blooms from late winter to mid-spring.

Fremontodendron 'California Glory' and *Euryops pectinatus*

The pond is colourful with water lilies and other flowering water plants and there are several varieties of fish. The walls around it are planted with alpines, bulbs, conifers, daphnes and other shrubs; there is also a small 'alpine meadow' at one corner and an area for moisture-loving herbaceous perennials. The bed at the east end of the pond is planted with a *Gunnera*, azaleas, hellebores, hardy *Cyclamen* and numerous bulbs. There is also a developing area of *Lathraea clandestina*, a parasite growing on the willow roots and only appearing above ground in early spring.

On the lawn a small island bed is backed by a border of mixed shrubs underplanted with *Cyclamen cilicium*. At the northern end is the Jubilee Garden, an alpine sink garden surrounded by mixed shrubs and summer-flowering plants.

In early spring the lilac bank, with *Cistus*, hostas and self-sown annuals, is carpeted with snowdrops, aconites and *Crocus tommasinianus* under an old ash, one of the six original trees.

Opposite: The island bed on the lawn brings together lupins, achilleas, osteospermums, poppies and *Euphorbia griffithii* among others

2

THE WOODLAND GARDEN

Developed from an old orchard, this is the only part of the garden where it is possible to grow rhododendrons, *Pieris*, camellias and magnolias successfully, although plantings of the last two have been made in several other areas as well. Magnolias here include *M. sprengeri* 'Diva', some *M.* × *soulangeana* forms and a hybrid raised at Hyde Hall from Nyman's seed. This tree is now 25ft (7.6m) high and has borne its highly scented flowers for some 15 years. It is believed to be a cross between *M. tripetala* and *M. hypoleuca*.

On entering the woodland visitors are greeted by the early-flowering *Cornus mas* with the deep rose pink form of *Cyclamen coum* seeding freely beneath it. Various species of *Helleborus* and their seedlings, daffodils and other bulbs, primulas, hostas, *Meconopsis*, hydrangeas, *Colchicum*, autumn-flowering *Crocus* and ferns, are all planted beneath the rhododendrons. These include a number of seedlings donated from various gardens in Scotland including some of the large-leaved species like the yellow-flowered *R. macabeanum* and the paler cream *R. sinogrande*, rarely seen in eastern England. A further range of attractive *Rhododendron* species and hybrids, *R. thomsonii, R. campanulatum, R. niveum, R. arboreum* and *R.* 'Shilsonii', also thrive and bloom freely here.

Taller maples, birches and *Eucalyptus gunnii*, planted in 1963 provide excellent shelter. A large *Cedrus atlantica* is underplanted with *Cyclamen hederifolium*.

Deciduous azaleas and hostas in the Woodland Garden

3

THE GOLD GARDEN

The Gold Garden was planted in 1978, replacing irises as this corner had become too shady for these sun-loving plants. Now bright again the gilding is furnished by yellow flowers and foliage, from the golden daffodils in spring to the conifers, still gold in autumn and winter. Other noteworthy plants are *Elaeagnus,* especially *E.* × *ebbingei* 'Gilt Edge' and *E. pungens* 'Frederici', *Cytisus battandieri, Philadelphus coronarius* 'Aureus' and the yellow long-lasting fruits of *Malus* 'Golden Hornet'.

Attractive foliage in the Gold Garden includes *Cortaderia* 'Gold Band', *Genista, Elaeagnus* and conifers

4

OLD ROSES

This long border contains many species and cultivars of old-fashioned and modern shrub roses. These give a rich range of colour, form and scent, followed in some cultivars by hips in the autumn. There is also variation in size and habit, from low ground-cover 'Nozomi' to tall shrubs like 'Nevada', 'Constance Spry' and the Alba group of roses. Many of them have one glorious season of flower, so to maintain interest throughout the year, other plants have been blended with them. These include *Prunus*, magnolias and *Rubus* 'Tridel' with a spring and early summer show of daffodils, leucojums and *Lilium candidum*. In June the tall pale pink spikes of *Eremurus robustus* provide a striking display towering above the roses. From the original six plants there are now hundreds of self-sown seedlings that flower profusely and are increasing each year.

Eremurus robustus in the shrub rose border

5

ROPE WALK AND MODERN ROSES

Modern roses 'Nozomi', 'The Fairy' and 'Angelina'

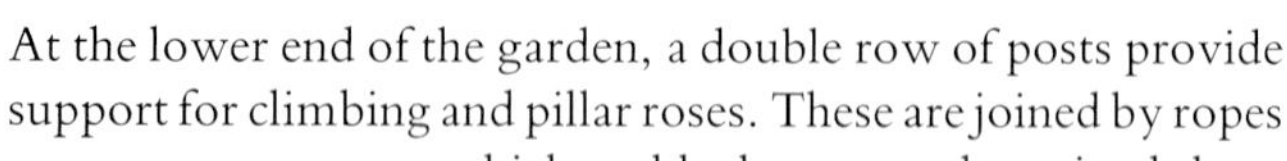

At the lower end of the garden, a double row of posts provide support for climbing and pillar roses. These are joined by ropes which enable the roses to be trained along them to intermingle with one another. *Clematis* are also planted and use the roses for support; between the posts, groups of modern bush roses blend with their taller neighbours to make a delightful midsummer walk. Stretching up the slope from here are seven large beds of modern roses, with two more at the top by the pond. The plantings are mainly in colour groups and they are periodically renewed with the best of the newer cultivars replacing some of the older ones.

6

IRISES AND THE PERENNIAL BORDERS

In late May and early June, if visitors turn left at the end of the Rope Walk to go beyond the yew hedge, they will find a glorious rainbow of modern tall and intermediate bearded irises that give pleasure both by colour and delightful scent.

A right turn at the end of the Rope Walk leads visitors along the mixed border which contains flowering shrubs and herbaceous perennials arranged in colour groups, separated by yew hedges. There is one break in the sequence in the central area where a peony collection provides an abundance of colour during June. At the upper end of the border there is a corner containing *Magnolia* × *loebneri* 'Merrill' underplanted with silver-blue *Juniperus squamata* 'Blue Carpet'. Further on is another small planting of shrubs and perennials by the black shed. Here the Golden Bay dominates, with a theme planting of silver and pastel shades around it.

Climbing roses along the Rope Walk, 'Santa Catalina', 'Chaplin's Pink Companion' and 'Iceberg'

7

THE WINTER GARDEN, HEATHER AND CONIFERS

At the lower end of the garden near the pond is a winter garden with a large bed of willows, stooled in the spring so that they grow during summer to provide coloured bark in the winter. This area is underplanted with *Galanthus* 'S. Arnott'. Nearby is a mixed planting of winter-flowering shrubs including winter jasmine grown as ground cover. The largest bed is planted with a range of slow-growing conifers; Hyde Hall has a large collection of these and they are especially valuable for winter effect, with their very considerable variation in shape, form and colour. More conifers are planted with the heathers, which are mainly cultivars of the winter-flowering *Erica carnea* and *E.* × *darleyensis*.

Beds of heathers *Erica* and *Calluna*, mostly winter-flowering

8

LOWER POND AND WATERFALL

Walk up, between the heathers and the conifers and then down the path by the waterfall. The narrow beds contain herbaceous plants, alpines, bulbs and shrubs, and at the bottom a stream passes a small alpine scree, to enter the lower pond. Around this pond, moisture-loving plants luxuriate, willows, dogwoods, astilbes, *Iris sibirica* forms, primulas and the large-leaved *Gunnera*. In the pond are native water-plants, including the beautiful flowering rush, *Butomus*, water lilies and the sweet-scented *Aponogeton distachyos*, water hawthorn.

The quiet seclusion of the lower pond with *Rosa* 'Felicia' behind

9

VIBURNUMS AND FLOWERING SHRUBS

The five beds above the lower pond include some trees (birch, cherry, magnolias, *Sorbus* and a fastigiate oak amongst them), but they are mainly devoted to shrubs, though the first has some modern *Hemerocallis* cultivars and in others there are *Agapanthus* hybrids and *Schizostylis*. The shrubs include azaleas, *Cotoneaster, Forsythia, Philadelphus, Hamamelis* and *Viburnum*. Much of the National Collection of *Viburnum* is to be found here and this has both a scientific purpose (conservation and study of the genus) and also shows their value as garden plants, with their wide range of flowers, leaves and fruits.

Opposite: The Miniature Rose Garden displays more than 50 cultivars

10

CONIFERS

The last bed in this area is planted with a number of choice slow-growing conifers including a collection of *Tsuga canadensis* forms.

THE MINIATURE ROSES

These raised beds are planted with many cultivars of miniature roses in a formal setting around a small paved area. In summer several containers are placed here, including those planted with cultivars of the New Zealand flax, *Phormium*. The narrow roadside border is planted with hardy nerines and *Ceratostigma willmottianum* for late summer colour.

THE BANK

Following the path across the upper side of the bank, visitors will see to the right a well-drained sunny bed for South African and European bulbs, especially *Amaryllis, Crinum, Nerine* and *Sternbergia*.

Amaryllis belladonna, one of several South African bulbs grown on the Bank

To the left and beyond the bank is shrubbery with trees underplanted with bulbs, daffodils, *Allium christophii* and *A. giganteum*.

Shrubs of note include *Abelia triflora, Dipelta floribunda, Mahonia aquifolium* 'Moseri' and *Staphylea colchica*. Among the trees is the beautiful foliaged *Gleditsia triacanthos* 'Sunburst' from the USA and *Salix matsudana* 'Tortuosa'. Further round, towards the Pig Park, is a bed of *Hemerocallis* cultivars.

13

CAR PARK

This is a large area of grass in which are planted broad-leaved trees including the latest additions to the National *Malus* Collection. There are several long avenues, the main one of *Acer saccharinum* and *A. rubrum*; others are planted with horse chestnuts, golden ash and limes. Groups of flowering trees are grown here and bordering the drive are *Malus* 'Golden Hornet' and 'John Downie', two good fruiting crab-apple cultivars. Along the entrance road is a shelter belt of *Pinus nigra*.

14

THE PIG PARK

Visitors who love trees and shrubs will find much to enjoy here. Some of the National Collection of *Malus* cultivars are planted in association with old-fashioned roses and other flowering shrubs and trees. On the right as you enter, are magnolias including *M. delavayi* and several cultivars of *M.* × *soulangeana* including 'Brozzonii', 'Burgundy' and 'Picture', the Scottish flame-flower *Tropaeolum speciosum*, growing rampantly amongst them. Continuing further round the barn, camellias and garryas have been provided with a north-facing, sheltered position. On the left of the entrance from the Car Park, the first bed contains the new English roses bred by David Austin; beyond it is a bed with magnolias, skimmias, the variegated form of *Rhamnus alaternus* and several different cultivars of the winter-flowering *Viburnum tinus*.

Ahead are two large beds of shrub roses, many of which have attractive fruits as well as their scented flowers, and to the left of the roses are beds planted with a variety of young trees.

Many of the *Malus* are excellent garden trees providing flower, fruit and often autumn colour as well. Some of the most garden-worthy selections planted here are 'Chilko', 'Almey', 'Katherine', 'Lady Northcliffe', 'Red Sentinel', 'Simcoe', with its copper-tinted young growth, and 'Van Eseltine' of columnar habit. *Malus transitoria*, a late-flowering species, has good autumn colour as well as yellow fruit.

The Pig Park, where the National Collection of *Malus* flowers in springtime and the fruits give colour in autumn

15

OFFICE BEDS AND FLAT

Leaving the Pig Park, and crossing the roadway, the visitor will see some fine *Cotoneaster horizontalis* on the building opposite and a 'Mermaid' rose on the wall. Passing behind the offices, the path leads by a shrubbery on the left which was one of the earliest plantings of summer-flowering shrubs – lilacs, shrub roses, some crab-apples and *Hibiscus syriacus* 'Blue Bird' and 'Woodbridge'.

STANDING GROUND

After the shrubbery, the path leads to the former kitchen garden enclosed by climbing roses and *Clematis*. Other plantings include a collection of slow-growing conifers. In a further section are dahlias and chrysanthemums and seedlings of other young plants being grown on before planting out in the main garden. Turning sharp right round the hedge, the bank on the left is planted with *Mahonia* × *media* cultivars to flower from November to April and underplanted with hardy *Cyclamen*.

HERMIONE'S GARDEN AND THE STABLE FLOOR

Named after the little statue of Hermione placed here, this shady area contains hydrangeas, hellebores, ivies and a number of ferns under an ash tree. Beside the steps *Prunus* 'Kursar' is also underplanted with *Cyclamen*. This cherry and an *Amelanchier* nearby give good autumn colour.

The border on the left of the lawn slopes up to the lilac bank and contains a number of cultivars of *Hydrangea paniculata* as well as many hellebores and bulbs.

To the left, the Tudor bricks of the ancient stable floor, uncovered many years ago, are now colonised by self-sown alpine aquilegias, anemones, cyclamen, pulsatillas and violas.

Opposite: Medieval brick paving interspersed with self-sown seedlings

18

THE TEA YARD

This paved area is enclosed on three sides by buildings and on the fourth by a low wall. Refreshments are available from the Essex Barn when the garden is open.

In this sheltered area are colourful containers. The borders display a number of semi-tender plants – salvias, abutilons, *Solanum crispum* 'Glasnevin', *Campsis radicans, R. banksiae* and *Viburnum macrocephalum.* There are also camellias, the South African *Melianthus* with its attractive large foliage providing a sub-tropical effect, and spreading along the low wall, smaller-flowered *Clematis. C. cirrhosa* var. *balearica* is planted against the south wall of the yard, near the tea-yard entrance and the end wall of the barn supports the rose 'Wedding Day'.

THE GREENHOUSES

A The Cool House – kept just free from frost by electronically controlled heating and ventilation. Planted here are climbers such as *Lapageria* and passion flower, *Passiflora* shrubs including *Abutilon,* camellias, buddlejas, *Clianthus, Datura,* fuchsias, the tree-fern *Dicksonia, Acacia baileyena* and *Pandorea jasminoides.*

B The Alpine House – staging on one side is used to display a changing variety of bulbs and alpines in pots. There is a raised bed on the other side.

C The Conservatory – a bright display of popular pot-plants on the staging, depending on the season.

A selection of seasonal plants is displayed in the Conservatory

ACKNOWLEDGEMENTS

Written by Christopher Brickell, CBE, VMH
Maps and design by John Fitzmaurice
Photographs by Harry Smith Photographic Collection
Copyright © 1994 The Royal Horticultural Society
ISBN 1-8744431-19-1